CLASS 08/09 LOCOMOTIVES

Andrew Cole

AMBERLEY

First published 2017

Amberley Publishing
The Hill, Stroud
Gloucestershire, GL5 4EP

www.amberley-books.com

Copyright © Andrew Cole, 2017

The right of Andrew Cole to be identified as
the Author of this work has been asserted in
accordance with the Copyrights, Designs and
Patents Act 1988.

ISBN 978 1 4456 6623 5 (print)
ISBN 978 1 4456 6624 2 (ebook)

British Library Cataloguing in Publication Data.
A catalogue record for this book is available from
the British Library.

Origination by Amberley Publishing.
Printed in the UK.

Introduction

The Class 08/09 locomotives were constructed from 1952 onwards at various British Railways workshops, including Crewe, Derby, Darlington, Doncaster and Horwich. Nearly 1,200 locos were built over a ten-year period; some were designated as Class 08, some as Class 09 and 146 as Class 10. This book concentrates on the Class 08s and 09s.

The Class 08 was the backbone of the British Railway shunting fleet, with nearly every corner of Britain home to one or more of the class. They could be found from Penzance to Inverness, and at all points in-between.

The class was fitted with an English Electric 6KT engine, capable of 350-hp power output. They were built to a 0-6-0 wheel configuration and were fitted with coupling rods.

They performed their duties faultlessly over the years; nevertheless, the work they were built for was soon to shrink, with the result that many were placed into storage. They would work at yards, and most stations had a pilot loco to shunt release locos, or to attach coaches. With the advent of multiple units, this work soon started to come to an end, with the class finding itself out of work. Another problem for the class were block freights, which didn't require shunting at yards; with the constriction of other freight flows, they soon found work in the large yards hard to come by.

Despite this, many of the class were still employed at depots and many were repainted into local liveries or, indeed, repainted back into liveries of old pre-nationalisation companies. Many depots took pride in their Class 08s, and adorned them with names and special liveries.

The class were also to find a home working on preserved railways, with their haulage capacity exploited on works trains and even on revenue-earning trains on the lines. Nearly seventy can be found up and down the country on preserved lines.

A large number of the class have been scrapped, with scrappings taking place at BREL Works and also carried out by private firms. Five class members were fitted with cut-down cabs to work the Burry Port & Gwendreath Valley line in South Wales. A further twelve locos were rebuilt as extra Class 09s by RFS at their Kilnhurst Works in 1992.

Five Class 08s were exported to Liberia in 1975, where they worked on the LAMCO Railway. The design was also sold abroad, with Australia and the Netherlands having batches of their own, although these were more similar to the Class 11.

The Class 09s differed from the Class 08s by having a different gearing; they were also equipped with a top speed of 27 mph. The majority of the class was based around the southern region and fitted with high-level air pipes to work with the southern EMUs. With their higher speed, the Class 09s proved popular on preserved lines, with a total of eleven preserved out of the twenty-six built.

Both classes can still be found hard at work today, at small yards, and also with private companies.

I have decided to list the photographs in pre-TOPS number order; hence some may seem to be out of sequence. The two different classes have also been split.

D3000, 5 October 2003

D3000 (No. 13000) stands outside Barrow Hill roundhouse, having been fully restored to original condition. This was the pioneer Class 08, and was the forerunner to a Class, combined with the Class 09 and 10, of over 1,000 engines. D3000 was built in 1952, and was sold for industrial use to the NCB before being successfully preserved.

D3011, 22 November 1981

D3011 (13011) is seen stabled at Tyseley depot, Birmingham. At the time D3011 had been withdrawn from British Rail service, and was in use at the British Leyland factory at Longbridge, Birmingham. It gained the name *Lickey*, as the factory was close to the Lickey Hills and famous incline. D3011 was scrapped by Marple & Gillott, Sheffield, in 1985.

No. 08008, 1 March 1981

No. 08008 (No. 13011, D3015) is seen acting as works pilot at Doncaster in the early 1980s. At the time, this was the second oldest Class 08 in regular use, and it would be withdrawn in 1983 and sent to Swindon Works for scrapping, which was completed in 1986.

No. 13029, 29 September 1998

No. 13029 (D3029, No. 08021) is seen preserved at Tyseley Railway Museum. The loco has been returned to BR black livery, and it also carries its original running number of 13029. This was later changed to D3029, and subsequently it was given the TOPS number No. 08021.

No. 08022, 30 May 2016

No. 08022 (No. 13030, D3030) is seen at Wallingford on the Cholsey & Wallingford Railway. This loco was withdrawn from British Rail service in 1985 and was sold to Guinness, Park Royal, to shunt at their works. It gained the large Guinness symbol on the front and rear, and also gained the name *Lion*. It, along with its sister loco No. 08060, which was also used by Guinness, were preserved at Cholsey.

No. 08060, 30 May 2016

No. 08060 (No. 13074, D3074) is seen preserved at Cholsey on the Cholsey & Wallingford Railway. This loco carries Guinness black livery as it was brought for preservation from Guinness, Park Royal. While working at Park Royal, No. 08060 received the name *Unicorn*.

No. 08068, 4 December 1983

No. 08068 (No. 13083, D3083) stands at Tyseley in withdrawn condition. This loco, along with classmate No. 08067, were long-term Midland Region residents, having both spent time allocated to Saltley. No. 08068 would be moved to Swindon Works for scrapping, which was completed in 1986.

D3090, 27 May 1967

D3090 (No. 13090, No. 08075) is seen working through Derby station, having not long been repainted into BR blue livery. I'm not sure if this was a test run from the nearby works, as it was allocated to Bescot at the time. D3090 was later renumbered as 08075, and was withdrawn from Shirebrook depot in 1981. It was then scrapped at Swindon Works in 1982.

No. 13101, 27 May 2016

No. 13101 (D3101) is seen stabled at Leicester depot on the Great Central Railway. This loco was withdrawn from British Rail service in 1972 and, as such, never received a TOPS number. It was sold to ARC at Loughborough, before being sold to the Great Central for preservation in 1984.

D3167, 10 August 2016

D3167 (No. 13167, No. 08102) is seen preserved at the Lincolnshire Wolds Railway, Ludborough. D3167 was withdrawn from service in 1988 and was bought by Lincoln City Council. It was plinthed outside Lincoln signal box in the early 1990s and then moved to the Lincolnshire Wolds Railway in 1994.

No. 08123, 30 May 2016

No. 08123 (No. 13190, D3190) is seen at Wallingford on the Cholsey & Wallingford Railway while undergoing repairs. This loco was brought for preservation directly by the Cholsey & Wallingford Railway in 1985, having been withdrawn from Crewe diesel depot.

No. 08141, 20 March 1988

No. 08141 (No. 13209, D3209) stands in the scrap line at Tinsley depot, having been withdrawn a couple of months earlier. This loco carries the unofficial name *Manvers*, and was one of many Tinsley-based engines to receive unofficial names. No. 08141 was later moved to Booth Roe Metals, Rotherham, for scrap, which was completed in 1994.

RFS 002, 12 July 1992

RFS 002 (No. 13232, D3232, No. 08164) is seen on display at Doncaster Works open day, 1992. The loco carries RFS livery, and also the number RFS 002. It had been renumbered from 08164, and while in RFS ownership it gained the name *Prudence*. RFS 002 was later sold to the East Lancashire Railway for preservation.

D3232, 8 September 2006

D3232 (No. 13232, No. 08164, RFS 002) is seen at Bury (Bolton Street) station on the East Lancashire Railway. This had been brought for preservation from RFS Industries, who had renumbered it RFS 002. This loco spent nearly all its working life in the North East, allocated to Gateshead, Hull and Darlington.

PO1, 26 October 1980

PO1 (No. 13241, D3241, No. 08173) is seen stabled at Polmadie depot, Glasgow. This had gained the internal number PO1 while based at Polmadie, although it was allocated to Eastfield at the time. However, it was renumbered back to 08173 in 1983, and was sold to Vic Berry for scrapping, which was completed at Thornton Junction in 1987.

No. 13265, 26 March 2016

No. 13265 (D3265, No. 08195) is seen stabled outside the main shed on the Llangollen Railway. The loco was withdrawn from Cardiff Canton in 1983, and was dumped at Swindon Works for a couple of years before being sold to the Llangollen Railway for preservation. The loco carries BR black livery, and also its original running number of 13265.

No. 08216, 27 June 1999

No. 08216 (No. 13286, D3286) is seen in preservation at the South Yorkshire Railway Preservation Society, Meadowhall. This loco was withdrawn from Derby in 1980 and sold to the Sheerness Steel Company for further use, moving to Kent in 1983. It was later sold into preservation but, as can be seen, it was in a derelict condition. It was later scrapped in 2001 to provide spare parts for other locos.

No. 08238, 30 July 2016

No. 08238 (No. 13308, D3308) is seen preserved at the Dean Forest Railway, Lydney. No. 08238 was originally withdrawn from Gloucester depot in 1984, and was sold for further use; it was employed at Swindon Railway Workshops from 1988 onwards. It later moved to the Dean Forest Railway, who applied the name *Charlie*.

No. 08258, 24 February 1987

No. 08258 (No. 13328, D3328) is seen at Peterborough while on station pilot duty. This would survive in service until 1988, when it was withdrawn from Cambridge depot and sold for scrap to Vic Berry, Leicester, who cut up the loco in 1989.

No. 08266, 29 August 2006

No. 08266 (No. 13336, D3336) is seen preserved at the Keighley & Worth Valley Railway. This loco spent the majority of its working life in Yorkshire, finally being withdrawn from Shirebrook depot in 1985. It was preserved by the K&WVR, and is seen carrying green livery but with its TOPS number, 08266, applied.

No. 08266, 22 August 2016

No. 08266 (No. 13336, D3336) is seen in the yard at Haworth on the Keighley & Worth Valley Railway. The loco has been superbly repainted into departmental grey livery, which is one that No. 08266 never carried. The loco carries a 55F depot plaque on the front, which is for Bradford Hammerton Street. Despite never carrying this livery, the repaint is excellent.

No. 97801, 13 April 1985

No. 97801 (No. 13337, D3337, No. 08267, RDB968020) is seen at Derby while in research use. This loco was withdrawn from Barrow Hill depot in 1977 and was transferred to the research department for use as a remote-control test loco; at this point it gained the name *Pluto*. It was withdrawn from use and then scrapped by Vic Berry, Leicester, in 1985.

No. 08295, 26 March 1989

No. 08295 (No. 13365, D3365) stands condemned at Thornaby depot, Teesside. This loco had been withdrawn nearly twelve months earlier, and would make the long journey south to Margam for scrapping, with Gwent Demolition scrapping the loco in 1993. No. 08295 carries British Steel stickers, so perhaps it had been on hire at some stage.

TS002, 16 January 1988

TS002 (D3367, No. 08297) is seen at Tyseley depot, Birmingham, carrying the number TS002 and an unusual white-and-black chevron livery on the front. This was an unusual renumbering, as it was only allocated to Tyseley for four months before being transferred away to Doncaster Carr. It was later sold to Vic Berry, Leicester, for scrap, and was cut up in 1990. As an aside, this was the first Class 08 delivered with a 'D' prefix.

No. 08305, 25 March 1989

No. 08305 (D3375) spends the weekend stabled at Crofton Permanent Way Yard, South Yorkshire, although official records have No. 08305 withdrawn in October 1988. It was stored at Knottingley depot, before being sold to Gwent Demolition, Margam, for scrap; it was cut up in 1995.

No. 08331, 21 November 2015

No. 08331 (D3401, RFS 001) is seen preserved at the Midland Railway Centre, Butterley. This is another Class 08 that was sold to RFS Industries for further use, this time renumbered as RFS 001 and carrying the name *Terence*. This loco spent many years hired to various different places, before being sold to the Midland Railway Centre for preservation in 2012.

No. 08335, 6 June 1987

No. 08335 (D3405) stands in the scrap line at Tinsley depot, Sheffield. This loco had been in collision with No. 20116 at the depot in January, and would be sold to Thomas Hill, Kilnhurst, as they were in the running for some Class 08 overhauls. It was later brought by RFS Industries, who sold the remains for scrap; they were cut up by C. F. Booth, Rotherham, at Kilnhurst in 1989.

No. 08345, 7 June 2009

No. 08345 (D3415) is seen at Long Marston, carrying plain yellow livery. This loco spent all its working life in Scotland, being withdrawn from Ayr depot in 1983. It was later sold to Deanside Transit, Glasgow, for use as an industrial shunter. It was later sold for scrap, and was cut up by C. F. Booth, Rotherham, in 2009.

No. 08401, 17 September 2016

No. 08401 (D3516) is seen at Hams Hall Distribution Park while on yard pilot duty. This loco carries green livery, and also Hunslet engine company logos on the battery box cover.

No. 08411, 14 August 1988

No. 08411 (D3526) is seen stabled at Thornaby depot, carrying BR blue livery. This loco, like many other Class 08s, led a fairly mundane life, before being withdrawn in 2004. It was later sold to Traditional Traction Limited.

No. 08411, 15 September 2015

We fast forward twenty-seven years from the previous photograph to see No. 08411 (D3526) at Rye Farm, Wishaw, in a very derelict condition, having been stripped for spare parts by Traditional Traction Limited. This loco will eventually be scrapped. Of note is the fact that it is fitted with a knuckle coupler to be able to shunt EWS coal hoppers, which aren't fitted with standard couplings.

No. 08414, 10 March 1996

No. 08414 (D3529) is seen at Ipswich while on yard pilot duty. This loco carries grey livery, and has also received its pre-TOPS number on the cabside. Also of note are the high-level air pipes, which were fitted when it was allocated to Ashford on the Southern Region. Despite the repaint, this loco would be sold to European Metal Recycling, Kingsbury, for scrap; it was cut up in 2007.

No. 08415, 20 November 1994

No. 08415 (D3530) is seen stabled at Ellesmere Port while on yard pilot duty. This loco was actually withdrawn in 1981, only to be reinstated to traffic in 1985 at Tyseley. It was withdrawn again, this time in 1996, but there was to be no second reprieve – this time it was scrapped by European Metal Recycling, Sheffield, in 1997.

No. 08419, 21 May 2000

No. 08419 (D3534) is seen in the scrap lines at Crewe Works during the open day of 2000. This was another loco that was withdrawn in 1981, moving to Swindon Works and held in storage. It was later reinstated to Carlisle Kingmoor, and was finally retired from service in 1993. It was later sold to Wabtec, who stripped it of all useful parts, before sending the remains to C. F. Booth, Rotherham, who scrapped it in 2004.

No. 08421, 26 March 1989

No. 08421 (D3536, No. 09201) spends the weekend stabled at Sunderland Docks depot. This was very much a steam age depot, which would unfortunately end up being demolished. No. 08421 would lead an uneventful life, being a Scottish-based Class 08 up until its last five years of service, when it moved to the North East. No. 08421 was rebuilt as No. 09201 by RFS Industries, Kilnhurst, in 1992.

No. 08441, 15 November 2015

No. 08441 (D3556) is seen undergoing restoration to mainline standards at Traditional Traction's base at Rye Farm, Wishaw. When completed, this loco moved to Bounds Green depot to take up depot pilot duty.

No. 08442, 11 April 1993

No. 08442 (D3557) stands at Knottingley depot while carrying unbranded Railfreight livery. Another Class 08 to lead an uneventful life, it was later moved to Eastleigh depot, and is in internal use there.

No. 08443, 5 September 1998

No. 08443 (D3558) is seen preserved at Bo'ness on the Bo'ness & Kinneil Railway. This loco spent all its life in Scotland, being withdrawn from Thornton Junction in 1985. It was then sold to DCL Scottish Grain Distillers for use at their Alloa works. It was later donated to the Bo'ness Railway in 1995.

No. 08448, 6 February 1991

No. 08448 (D3563) departs Washwood Heath yard with a single TTA fuel wagon for the nearby Saltley depot. This was another Class 08 that spent most of its life in Scotland, before transferring to Bescot in 1990. It was later sold to European Metal Recycling, Kingsbury, who scrapped the loco in 2007.

No. 08460, 23 August 2016

No. 08460 (D3575) is seen in the early stages of refurbishment at Traditional Traction's Rye Farm base. No. 08460 spent a lot of its working life on the old Great Eastern, being based at Stratford, Norwich and Colchester depots, before finding its way to the North West in 1997.

No. 08994, 15 September 2015

No. 08994 (D3577, No. 08462) sits on the back of a low loader at Traditional Traction's yard at Rye Farm, Wishaw. This loco was originally numbered 08462, and was rebuilt with a cut-down cab in 1987 to work the Burry Port & Gwendreath Valley line in South Wales; it was one of five Class 08s to be converted. Three of the five locos were later transferred to ordinary duties, while Nos 08991 and 08992 were scrapped. No. 08994 can today be found at Nemesis Rail's depot at Burton-on-Trent.

No. 08466, 20 May 1989

No. 08466 (D3581) is seen stabled at Tyseley carrying original Railfreight livery, complete with large numbers on the battery box cover. This was another Class 08 that was withdrawn for a couple of years in the early 1980s, before being reinstated to Bescot. It would eventually be scrapped by C. F. Booth, Rotherham, in 2011.

No. 08472, 4 July 1996

No. 08472 (D3587) is seen at Alexandra Palace while on depot pilot duty at the nearby Bounds Green depot. No. 08472 is shunting some of the Charter Stock Mk I carriages. Today, No. 08472 can still be found shunting at an East Coast depot at Edinburgh Craigentinny.

No. 08482, 2 April 2009

No. 08482 (D3597) is seen employed on yard pilot duty at Eastleigh, carrying EWS maroon livery. No. 08482 carries the name *Don Gates 1962–2000*, and would be sold for scrap; it was sent to C. F. Booth, Rotherham, who scrapped the loco in 2011.

No. 08484, 15 September 2015

No. 08484 (D3599) is seen at Traditional Tractions Rye Farm yard, carrying plain blue livery and the name *Captain Nathaniel Darrell*. This loco spent many years based at Wolverton Works as a works pilot before being sold to the Port of Felixstowe, in whose blue livery it is seen. It was later sold on to Traditional Traction.

No. 08489, 25 May 1998

No. 08489 (D3604) is seen in storage at Warrington Arpley Yard. This loco carries unbranded Railfreight grey livery and carries the unofficial name *Billy Boy*. No. 08489 would eventually be sold for scrap to T. J. Thomson, Stockton, who scrapped the loco in 2009.

D3605, 17 September 2015

D3605 (No. 08490) is seen preserved at Aviemore on the Strathspey Railway. Another class member to lead an unremarkable career, No. 08490 was withdrawn from Thornton Junction in 1985 and has spent the last thirty years in preservation.

No. 08492, 9 July 2006

No. 08492 (D3607) is seen in long-term storage at Barrow Hill. This had been withdrawn from Motherwell depot and sold to Harry Needle for spares recovery. It was later sold to European Metal Recycling, Kingsbury, for scrap, and it was cut up in 2012.

No. 08506, 14 August 1988

No. 08506 (D3661) spends the weekend stabled outside the main shed at Thornaby depot, Teesside. This loco carries BR blue livery, offset with a red solebar. No. 08506 would eventually be scrapped by T. J. Thomson, Stockton, in 2007.

No. 08509, 25 March 1989

No. 08509 (D3664) is seen stabled at Tinsley depot, Sheffield, having just been repainted into Railfreight grey livery. No. 08509 also carries the unofficial name *Wath ETD*. No. 08509 was scrapped by C. F. Booth, Rotherham, in 2009.

No. 08510, 20 March 2003

No. 08510 (D3672) trundles through Doncaster station, carrying BR blue livery, with a rake of Network Rail ballast wagons. No. 08510 carries the unofficial name *Canklow*, and would be scrapped by C. F. Booth, Rotherham, in 2009.

No. 08511, 11 December 2015

No. 08511 (D3673) is seen stored at Traditional Traction's yard at Rye Farm, Wishaw. This loco carries former EWS maroon livery but has had the EWS logo replaced with a Traditional Traction logo.

No. 08514, 23 August 2007

No. 08514 (D3676) is seen running through Doncaster station while hauling a twin jib crane. Despite wearing EWS maroon livery, No. 08514 would be scrapped by European Metal Recycling, Kingsbury, in 2011.

No. 08529, 3 July 1996

No. 08529 (D3691) approaches Peterborough with an engineers' train. Of note is the headlamp carried on the loco front. No. 08529 would go on to be withdrawn in 1999, and was scrapped by C. F. Booth, Rotherham, in 2008.

No. 08536, 15 April 2016

No. 08536 (D3700) is seen condemned at RVEL Derby. This loco was withdrawn in 1995 and was stored in the old weighbridge at Etches Park until it was decided to demolish the building. No. 08536 was removed and taken across to RVEL for further storage.

No. 08540, 27 March 1991

No. 08540 (D3704) is seen running light engine through Peterborough station, having just been released from works overhaul, including a repaint into departmental grey livery. No. 08540 was withdrawn in 2004 and would be scrapped by European Metal Recycling, Kingsbury, in 2010.

No. 08562, 12 July 1992

No. 08562 (D3729) is seen stored at Doncaster Works carrying the name *The Doncaster Postman*. No. 08562 would find further use on Channel Tunnel construction trains until it was stored at Old Oak Common. It would be cut up on site by private contractors in 1997.

No. 08573, 20 June 1999

No. 08573 (D3740) is seen stabled at Ilford depot, carrying plain white livery. Today, No. 08573 is still employed as depot pilot at Ilford and retains its white livery.

No. 08585, 21 May 2000

No. 08585 (D3752) is seen acting as yard pilot at Crewe Basford Hall while carrying BR blue livery. Today, this loco can be found at Trafford Park, working for Freightliner.

No. 08586, 1 May 1993

No. 08586 (D3753) is seen stabled at Ayr depot, carrying unbranded Railfreight livery. This loco would only have another three years of service left, before being withdrawn in 1996. It was cut up in 2000 on site at Ayr.

No. 08588, 25 September 1995

No. 08588 (D3755) runs light engine through Leeds while carrying BR blue livery, but has a red solebar and white roof. Today No. 08588 is owned by ECT Mainline Rail and can be found shunting at the Cemex sleeper factory, Washwood Heath.

No. 08590, 20 September 2009

No. 08590 (D3757) is seen preserved at the Midland Railway Centre, Butterley. This loco carries BR blue livery and has also been named *Red Lion*, an unofficial name it carried when allocated to Bescot in the late 1970s. No. 08590 was withdrawn from Heaton depot before entering preservation.

No. 08993, 22 August 2016

No. 08993 (D3759, No. 08592) stands in the depot yard at Haworth on the Keighley & Worth Valley Railway. No. 08993 was rebuilt from No. 08592 in 1985 at Landore for use on the Burry Port & Gwendreath Valley line by having a cut-down cab fitted. No. 08993 carries the name *Ashburnham* and has been preserved carrying EWS maroon livery, which looks superb.

D3760, 10 March 1996

D3760 (No. 08593) is seen stabled at Harwich Parkeston Quay. The loco had been repainted at Stratford depot into black livery, lined with red and also carrying its pre-TOPS number, D3760. No. 08593 would eventually lose its special livery in favour of EWS maroon and was sold to Traditional Traction as a source of spares.

No. 08598, 23 August 2016

No. 08598 (D3765) is seen stabled at the Chasewater Railway, Brownhills. No. 08598 carries The Potter Group yellow livery. This had been withdrawn from Crewe depot in 1986.

No. 604, 28 May 2016

No. 604 (D3771, No. 08604) is seen preserved at the Didcot Railway Centre, carrying green livery. This was painted in green when it was allocated to Tyseley, and it is also seen carrying a cast number plate. It carries the name *Phantom*, which it gained while at Tyseley.

No. 08616, 23 January 1991

No. 08616 (D3783) passes through Washwood Heath, hauling classmate No. 08543 *Rotherwood* towards Saltley depot. Today No. 08616 can still be found in Birmingham, working for London Midland at Tyseley depot. As an aside, No. 08616 was the last locomotive overhauled at Swindon Works before its closure.

D3783, 15 January 1995

D3783 (No. 08616) is seen at Tyseley depot, Birmingham, having just been repainted into GWR green livery. Tyseley had a reputation for turning out its shunters in unusual liveries. No. 08616 is still allocated to Tyseley today, working for London Midland.

No. 08622, 8 July 2000

No. 08622 (D3789) is seen withdrawn at Motherwell depot, carrying BR blue livery. This had been withdrawn four years previously, but would be sold to RMS Locotec; it now earns a living at Ketton cement works.

No. 08623, 19 January 2014

No. 08623 (D3790) is seen stabled at Bescot halfway through a repaint into the latest DB Schenker red livery. This loco has been a long-time Midlands-based loco, being allocated to Derby, Toton, Leicester and Bescot, among other depots. This loco is now in storage at Bescot but, like most DB-owned Class 08s, it is for sale.

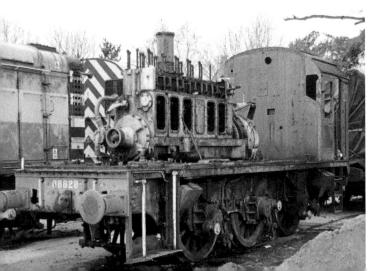

No. 08628, 11 December 2015

No. 08628 (D3795) is seen at Traditional Traction's yard at Rye Farm, Wishaw. The remains of this loco were at Rye Farm for spares recovery; it was scrapped by European Metal Recycling, Kingsbury, in May 2016.
No. 08628 had been withdrawn from Saltley depot in 1999.

No. 08630, 28 August 1996

No. 08630 (D3797) is seen stabled at Fort William depot carrying BR blue livery. This was taken at the time when the BR logo was being painted over on many of the locomotives on the network. No. 08630 is still in use today, working at Celsa Steel, Cardiff.

No. 08631, 29 September 1998

No. 08631 (D3798) is seen on one of the turntable roads at Tyseley Railway Museum. No. 08631 carries Network South East livery, a scheme not carried by many Class 08s. Today this can be found at Crewe LNWR.

No. 08632, 26 March 2014

No. 08632 (D3799) is seen stabled at Bescot, carrying EWS maroon livery. This was one of the Class 08s that were fitted with remote-control equipment, as indicated by the extra lights on the loco front. This now works at Mossend Yard, but is up for sale.

No. 08632, 6 June 2014

No. 08632 (D3799) sparkles in the summer sunshine at Bescot depot, having just been released from the depot. This had been repainted into DB Schenker red livery at Bescot, before it headed off to Mossend Yard to resume shunting duty.

No. 08635, 17 August 1986

No. 08635 (D3802) is seen stabled at Northwich depot, carrying BR blue livery. This had once been a Saltley-based loco; it was stored there for over twelve months in the early 1980s, before being reinstated in 1984. No. 08635 was preserved at the Severn Valley Railway.

No. 08644, 6 August 1995

No. 08644 (D3811) rests at Penzance, carrying InterCity livery. This has spent most of its life working in the West Country, based at both Penzance and Laira, where it is still allocated today.

No. 08645, 12 August 1987

No. 08645 (D3812) is seen acting as station pilot at Penzance while carrying BR blue livery. This is another Class 08 that has spent most of its working life based in the West Country. It is seen carrying the unofficial name *Friary*.

No. 08647, 18 March 1990

No. 08647 (D3814) is seen at Doncaster Works acting as a works pilot. The loco carries the name *Crimpsall* and green livery. No. 08647 was a Midlands-based loco for many years, including stints at Tyseley and Saltley, before it was sold to Doncaster BRML for use as their pilot. It would eventually be sold to the South Yorkshire Railway Preservation Society and moved to Meadowhall, where it was scrapped in 1997.

No. 08650, 11 December 2015

No. 08650 (D3817) is seen at Traditional Traction's Rye Farm yard while undergoing repairs. This loco is owned by Aggregate Industries and, upon completion of the repairs, it went back to work at Whatley Quarry. Note the extra air pipes fitted from when it was based at Ashford.

No. 08653, 3 March 1991

No. 08653 (D3820) rests outside Marylebone depot, London, carrying BR blue livery. This is another Class 08 fitted with extra air pipes from when it was allocated to Selhurst. Today the depot has been demolished to make way for a development of flats, while No. 08653 can be found stored at Barrow Hill, carrying EWS maroon livery.

No. 08655, 16 August 1999

No. 08655 (D3822) passes Milford Junction, hauling a rake of MGR wagons. The loco carries BR blue livery, but has had the BR logo replaced with a Railfreight Speedlink logo. Again, No. 08655 carries extra air pipes from when it was allocated to Selhurst. No. 08655 was scrapped by a private contractor at Barton-under-Needwood in 2007.

No. 08662, 16 January 2007

No. 08662 (D3829) passes light engine through Doncaster station, carrying EWS maroon livery. This loco was withdrawn in 2008, and would be scrapped by T. J. Thomson, Stockton, in 2012.

No. 08669, 6 August 2009

No. 08669 (D3836) is seen working outside Doncaster Works while carrying Wabtec Rail black livery. This was withdrawn from BR service in 1989 and sold to Trafford Park Estates for further use in Manchester. It was sold to Wabtec Rail in 2000, and carries the name *Bob Machin*.

No. 08670, 25 March 2016

No. 08670 (D3837) is seen acting as depot pilot at Bounds Green while carrying Railway Support Services livery. This loco is owned by Traditional Traction and is based at Bounds Green. No. 08670 spent many years based at Stratford before it headed to Motherwell.

No. 08682, 10 July 1994

No. 08682 (D3849) is seen at Doncaster Works while on Works pilot duty. It was owned by Adtranz at the time and carried the name *Lionheart*. It has since been since been sold to Bombardier and has moved to Derby Litchurch Lane.

No. 08995, 15 September 2015

No. 08995 (D3854, No. 08687) is seen in storage at Traditional Traction's Rye Farm yard. This was the last cut-down Class 08 to be rebuilt and it was converted from No. 08687 at Landore in 1987. This has been sold to the Shillingstone Railway Project, but is in storage at Wishaw.

No. 08690, 24 August 1995

No. 08690 (D3857) runs light engine past Derby station, carrying BR blue livery. This loco is still in use today with East Midlands Trains, but is based at Neville Hill depot, Leeds.

No. 08699, 21 May 2000

No. 08699 (D3866) is seen at Crewe Works during the open day of 2000. This loco carries plain-blue livery, as at the time it was owned by Adtranz. It was later sold to British American Railway services, and can be found on the Weardale Railway.

No. 08703, 22 March 1986

No. 08703 (D3870) is seen carrying BR blue livery at Crewe diesel depot. There was always a large allocation of 08s at Crewe to work the depot and nearby yards. Today No. 08703 is owned by DB Cargo, and can be found at Bescot carrying EWS maroon livery, although, like all DB Cargo shunters, it is for sale.

No. 08704, 10 March 2015

No. 08704 (D3871) is seen on depot pilot duty at Crewe diesel depot. Locomotive Services LTD now operates this depot, and No. 08704 is seen wearing Riviera Trains blue livery. No. 08704 can today be found at Nemesis Rail's depot at Burton-on-Trent.

No. 08707, 3 June 1993

No. 08707 (D3874) is seen being hauled through Doncaster station by No. 56067, while on its way to Doncaster Carr depot. No. 08707 was withdrawn the following month and sold to Harry Needle. After initially being stored at Meadowhall, Sheffield, it moved to Carnforth, where it would be scrapped in 2005.

No. 08719, 1 June 1988

No. 08719 (D3887) is seen stabled at York LIP along with classmate No. 08567. No. 08719 was later transferred to Bletchley, and from there it was withdrawn in 1991. It would make the journey to Margam for scrapping, being completed by Gwent Demolition in 1994.

No. 08721, 16 April 2016

No. 08721 (D3889) is seen at Bury (Bolton Street) on the East Lancashire Railway. This loco is owned by Alstom, and is usually based at Longsight for depot pilot duty, but was attending a shunter event on the East Lancs Railway. No. 08721 carries the name *Longsight TMD*.

No. 08728, 7 June 2009

No. 08728 (D3896) is seen in storage at Long Marston carrying Deanside Transit logos. No. 08728 had been withdrawn from Motherwell in 1987, and was sold direct to Deanside Transit for shunting at their premises. It later passed to Harry Needle, who sent it to C. F. Booth, Rotherham, for scrapping, which was completed in 2009.

No. 08730, 3 September 1994

No. 08730 (D3898) shunts a single parcels van around Springburn Works while carrying departmental grey livery. This loco was sold to Rail Maintenance Limited who operated Springburn Works at the time in 1994. Today No. 08730 still earns its keep at Springburn, but is now owned by Knorr Bremse Rail Systems.

No. 08734, 4 July 1993

No. 08734 (D3902) spends the weekend stabled at Tyseley depot alongside the newly built heavy cleaning shed. This loco was eventually sold privately and moved to the Dean Forest Railway, although it was stripped of all salvageable parts and subsequently scrapped by Sims Metals at Newport in 2011.

No. 08736, 7 June 2009

No. 08736 (D3904) is seen in storage at Long Marston carrying BR blue livery, but with Deanside Transit logos. This was another Class 08 withdrawn in 1987, and was sold to Deanside Transit to work at their premises at Hillington in Glasgow. It would be scrapped by C. F. Booth, Rotherham, five months later.

No. 08737, 27 March 1993

No. 08737 (D3905) is seen stabled at Crewe diesel depot carrying unbranded Railfreight livery. No. 08737 was later fitted with multiple working equipment and painted into EWS livery, but today it is withdrawn at Crewe electric depot.

No. 08742, 27 March 1993

No. 08742 (D3910) is seen side on at Crewe electric depot, while coupled to an OHLE cable drum-carrying wagon. No. 08742 is still active in the EWS fleet, being based at Oxford Hinksey Yard.

No. 08742, 28 May 2016

No. 08742 (D3910) stands in company with (08)604 at Didcot Railway Centre during their gala event. No. 08742 is remote-control fitted, as can be seen from the extra lights on the front. No. 08742 carries very faded Rail Express Systems livery, and is still in use at Oxford Hinksey Yard.

No. 08746, 26 December 1989

No. 08746 (D3914) spends Christmas 1989 stabled on the fuel tank line at Saltley. No. 08746 was eventually sold to Harry Needle, who sent it to C. F. Booth, Rotherham, for scrap in 2004.

No. 08762, 18 April 2013

No. 08762 (D3930) is seen at the Cemex Works at Washwood Heath, carrying black livery. This loco spent all of its life working in Scotland up until 1999, when it was sold to RT Rail Tours. This loco is now owned by ECT Mainline Rail and is currently stored at RVEL Derby.

No. 08765, 13 July 1986

No. 08765 (D3933) acts as yard pilot at Bescot, carrying BR blue livery but with yellow cab sides. This view also shows the rubber skirt fitted to protect the running gear; this is from when it was based at Oxley and used regularly through the carriage wash.

No. 08765, 29 December 1991

No. 08765 (D3933) carries departmental grey livery while on depot pilot duty at Tyseley. This loco spent many years based in the West Midlands, only venturing further afield in 2001 when it was transferred to Toton. Today this can be found at Barrow Hill in storage and is owned by Harry Needle.

D3935, 20 July 2006

D3935 (No. 08767) stands in the yard at Sheringham on the North Norfolk Railway. This loco was withdrawn from Stratford depot in 1994 and was preserved at the NNR, who restored it with its pre-TOPS number.

No. 08768, 3 September 1994

No. 08768 (D3936) is seen stabled at Carlisle Upperby depot while on depot shunting duty. This loco would be withdrawn from Motherwell in 2000, before being sold to T. J. Thomson, Stockton, for scrap, who cut the loco in 2007.

D3937, 30 July 2016

D3937 (No. 08769) stands at Norchard on the Dean Forest Railway. This loco was withdrawn in 1989 and sold to the fire service for use at their Moreton-in-Marsh training college. It was eventually brought for preservation and moved to the Dean Forest in 2000. It has been superbly restored back into BR green livery, and carries the name *Gladys*.

No. 08770, 14 August 1988

No. 08770 (D3938) is seen stabled at Thornaby depot, Teesside, carrying Railfreight General User livery. It also carries a Kingfisher depot sticker. There were not too many locos that carried these decals on the Railfreight grey livery. No. 08770 would be scrapped by T. J. Thomson, Stockton, in 2011.

D3940, 20 July 2006

D3940 (No. 08772) is seen at Weybourne on the North Norfolk Railway while carrying BR green livery. No. 08772 was withdrawn from Stratford depot in 1994, before being preserved at the North Norfolk Railway.

No. 08775, 14 June 1998

No. 08775 (D3943) rests at Hither Green depot, carrying BR blue livery; unusually it has a white cab roof and also large numbers on the battery box cover. This loco would be scrapped by C. F. Booth, Rotherham, in 2009.

No. 08776, 11 April 1993

No. 08776 (D3944) is seen stabled at Knottingley depot, carrying departmental grey livery. This was to be another loco scrapped by C. F. Booth, Rotherham, this time in 2011.

No. 08777, 8 September 1983

No. 08777 (D3945) is seen being hauled past Saltley depot, Birmingham, on its way from overhaul at Swindon Works back to its home depot of Hull Botanical Gardens. At the time this was how Class 08s were transported around the network; nowadays it's all done by low loader. No. 08777 was scrapped by C. F. Booth, Rotherham, in 1996.

No. 08782, 31 March 1997

No. 08782 (D3950) is seen stabled at Knottingley depot, carrying BR blue livery. Today No. 08782 still works for DB Cargo at Doncaster, but is currently up for sale.

No. 08786, 18 September 1999

No. 08786 (D3954) is seen at Plymouth while on Pathfinder Railtour duty. This loco worked, while top and tail with No. 09008, from Plymouth to Friary Sidings, and then onto the Cattewater Branch. No. 08786 is currently stored at Barrow Hill and is owned by Harry Needle.

No. 08788, 22 July 1993

No. 08788 (D3956) shunts the brand new No. 323202 out of the RTC at Derby, complete with No. 47972 attached to the rear, ready for onward movement. No. 08788 carries BR blue livery and is still in use today, working for British American Railway Services. It is based at Shotton Steel Works.

No. 08795, 4 August 1996

No. 08795 (D3963) acts as yard pilot at Swansea Maliphant sidings. This loco carries InterCity Mainline livery, which suited the loco well. No. 08795 has never strayed far from the South West, and today it works for Great Western Railway while still based at Landore, Swansea.

No. 08799, 6 August 2000

No. 08799 (D3967) is seen stabled at Acton Yard while on yard pilot duty. This loco has suffered a graffiti attack, and looks dreadful. It is still in use today, being a DB Cargo locomotive based at Westbury.

No. 08800, 29 June 1991

No. 08800 (D3968) is seen stabled at Bristol Bath Road during the depot's open day in 1991. No. 08800 carries InterCity Swallow livery, but was scrapped by Gwent Demolition, Margam, in 1994.

No. 08801, 9 August 1987

No. 08801 (D3969) is seen acting as yard pilot at St Blazey Depot, Cornwall. The 08 was based here to shunt china clay wagons. No. 08801 would be scrapped by C. F. Booth, Rotherham, in 2004.

No. 3973, 26 February 1995

No. 3973 (D3973, No. 08805) is seen stabled at Tyseley carriage sidings, having been repainted into LMS maroon livery. Tyseley always had a good reputation for the excellent repaints it did on its shunter allocation. No. 3973 carries the name *Concorde*, and today it can be found at London Midland's Soho depot.

No. 08813, 16 March 1997

No. 08813 (D3981) spends the weekend stabled at Thornaby depot, Teesside. To the left of the loco is where the roundhouse used to be. No. 08813 carries departmental grey livery, and was scrapped by T. J. Thomson, Stockton, in 2011.

No. 08814, 31 May 1991

No. 08814 (D3982) shunts No. 143609 at Derby, complete with ferry vans acting as translator vans. No. 08814 carries BR blue livery, and was scrapped by Gwent Demolition, Margam, in 1994.

No. 08818, 7 October 2001

No. 08818 (D3986) is seen under repair inside Barrow Hill roundhouse. No. 08818 carries Harry Needle orange livery, and today can be found earning its keep at Celsa Steel, Cardiff.

No. 08823, 25 October 2014

No. 08823 (D3991) shunts intermodal wagons at Daventry. The loco carries Malcolm Rail livery and the name *Libbie*. This loco still works at Daventry today.

No. 08824, 12 July 1992

No. 08824 (D3992) is seen at Doncaster station, carrying Railfreight General User livery. This was the day of the nearby works open day. No. 08824 is today owned by Harry Needle and is at Barrow Hill, but carries the number IEMD001 from when it was allocated to Crewe electric depot.

No. 08827, 3 September 1994

No. 08827 (D3995) spends the weekend stabled behind Carlisle Citadel station while carrying BR blue livery. There was always a large allocation of Class 08s allocated to Carlisle to work the yards and depots. No. 08827 was scrapped by European Metal Recycling, Kingsbury, in 2011.

No. 08830, 21 May 2000

No. 08830 (D3998) stands on display at Crewe Works open day, having been repainted into LNWR black livery. This loco carries additional air pipes from when it was allocated to Ashford and Eastleigh. Today, it has been preserved and it can be found at Peak Rail.

No. 08832, 2 December 1989

No. 08832 (D4000, No. 09102) rests at its home depot of Tyseley. This loco carries original Railfreight livery, but has had two white stripes added. This was originally numbered D4000, and would go on to be rebuilt as No. 09102 by RFS Industries, Kilnhurst, in 1992.

No. 08841, 4 February 1989

No. 08841 (D4009) is seen stabled outside the factory at Tyseley depot. This 08 carries BR blue livery, but also has a rubber skirt fitted to protect the running gear from its time shunting carriages through the wash at Oxley depot. No. 08841 would be scrapped by M. C. Metals, Glasgow, in 1993.

No. 08842, 12 July 1992

No. 08842 (D4010) is seen stabled at Doncaster yard, having had attention to its chassis – note the lack of connecting rods. No. 08842 would later be scrapped by European Metal Recycling, Kingsbury, in 2012.

No. 003, 15 September 2015

No. 003 (D4014, No. 08846) rests at Traditional Traction's yard at Rye Farm, Wishaw. This loco carries Bombardier blue livery and also their number, 003. This had been based at Derby Works since 1990 and was visiting Wishaw for repairs.

No. 08850, 22 August 1987

No. 08850 (D4018) is seen acting as depot pilot at Oxford. This is another Class 08 that received extra air pipes from when it was allocated to Eastleigh. This has since been preserved at the North Yorkshire Moors Railway.

No. 08865, 8 December 2012

No. 08865 (D4033) shunts ballast wagons at Bescot while on yard pilot duty. This loco carries EWS maroon livery, and has since been sold to Harry Needle; it can be found at Barrow Hill.

No. 08867, 22 August 1993

No. 08867 (D4035) *Ralph Easby* is seen stabled at its home depot of Thornaby. This loco had been repainted into black livery and had also received a Kingfisher depot sticker. No. 08867 would be scrapped by T. J. Thomson, Stockton, in 2007.

No. 08869, 7 June 2009

No. 08869 (D4037) is seen at Long Marston while in storage. This Class 08 carries green livery from when it was allocated to Norwich. No. 08869 was withdrawn with fire damage and would be scrapped by European Metal Recycling, Kingsbury, in 2011.

No. 08871, 6 August 2009

No. 08871 (D4039) is seen inside Wabtec Rails Works at Doncaster. This loco carries Cotswold Rail silver livery, which suited the loco well. Today this earns its keep at Trostre Steel.

No. 08873, 12 November 2013

No. 08873 (D4041) is seen on yard pilot duty at Hams Hall Distribution Park. This loco carries former RES livery, but has had Hunslet Engine Company logos applied on the battery box cover.

No. 08875, 26 March 1989

No. 08875 (D4043) is seen stabled at Thornaby depot, Teesside. This loco carries BR blue livery, complete with white roof and red buffer beam. This was sold to RFS Industries as a source of spare parts and was cut up at Kilnhurst in 1993.

No. 08876, 28 July 1984

No. 08876 (D4044) is seen on the back of a railtour at Doncaster station on the day of the nearby Works open day. This was the Plant Invader Railtour, which started at London Waterloo. No. 08876 was scrapped at RFS Doncaster in 1994.

No. 08879, 27 May 1996

No. 08879 (D4047) *Sheffield Children's Hospital* is seen stabled outside the shed at its home depot of Tinsley. This loco carries a special livery, which was applied at Tinsley in connection with the depot open day the previous month. No. 08879 is currently stored at Toton.

No. 08882, 1 September 1994

No. 08882 (D4096) is seen stabled at Aberdeen depot, carrying BR blue livery. On this day there was a strike by signalmen, so nothing was moving across the network. No. 08882 would be scrapped by Ron Hull Jr, Rotherham, in 2005.

No. 08884, 30 April 2000

No. 08884 (D4098) is seen stabled at Saltley depot, Birmingham, carrying BR blue livery. This loco carries the unofficial name *Saltley Seagulls* above the BR double arrow. No. 08884 would be scrapped by European Metal Recycling, Kingsbury, in 2010.

No. 08887, 14 March 1976

No. 08887 (D4117) is seen stabled at Allerton depot, carrying BR green livery but with its TOPS number applied. No. 08887 had been renumbered two years earlier, but still clung onto its green livery.

No. 08887, 3 February 1991

No. 08887 (D4117) spends the weekend stabled at Old Oak Common depot along with other classmates. No. 08887 carries BR blue livery and is still in use today, owned by Alstom.

No. 08888, 2 May 2015

No. 08888 (D4118) is seen stabled at Bescot, along with classmate 08907. No. 08888 is equipped with remote-control equipment, with the extra lights visible on the cab front. The loco also carries a broader yellow band on the EWS livery, again denoting it is remote-control fitted. No. 08888 can today be found working at Hoo Junction, but is up for sale.

No. 08896, 10 September 1998

No. 08896 (D4126) is seen acting as station pilot at Bristol Temple Meads. No. 08896 carries EWS maroon livery and also the name *Stephen Dent*. No. 08896 would be preserved at the Severn Valley Railway.

No. 08897, 22 August 1990

No. 08897 (D4127) runs light engine through Bristol Temple Meads, carrying departmental grey livery. At this time there was plenty of parcels traffic at Bristol to keep the resident pilot busy, but unfortunately most of this traffic was lost. No. 08897 was scrapped by C. F. Booth, Rotherham, in 2011.

No. 08898, 26 December 1990

No. 08898 (D4128) is seen condemned at Bescot. This loco was unsuccessfully used on the Burry Port & Gwendreath Valley line in South Wales, where it struck a low bridge, resulting in its withdrawal. The BP&GV line used to utilise the special cut-down Class 08/09s. No. 08898 would be scrapped at RFS Industries, Doncaster, in 1998.

No. 08899, 15 April 2016

No. 08899 (D4129) is seen stabled at Derby Etches Park, carrying Midland Railway livery. This loco was specially repainted by East Midlands Trains and also carries the name *Midland Counties Railway 175 1839–2014*.

No. 08903, 10 July 1994

No. 08903 (D4133) spends the weekend stabled at Tinsley, carrying BR blue livery. No. 08903 would be sold for industrial use, ending up working for Enron at their Wilton Works on Teesside.

No. 08904, 5 August 1990

No. 08904 (D4134) is seen stabled outside the office block at Marylebone depot. This loco is still in use today with DB Cargo and is based at Eastleigh. The depot at Marylebone was demolished and blocks of flats are now on the site.

No. 08907, 7 April 2014

No. 08907 (D4137) is seen acting as yard pilot at Bescot. This loco had not long been repainted into what was then DB Schenker livery; however, there has since been a name change and this loco now works for DB Cargo. It can still be found at Bescot.

No. 08908, 7 September 1991

No. 08908 (D4138) is seen on station pilot duty at Leeds. The loco is seen at the old parcels sidings but, with the loss of parcels traffic, this area has now been rebuilt as extra platforms. No. 08908 has been allocated to Neville Hill depot since 1987, but now works for East Midlands Trains.

No. 08912, 30 August 1996

No. 08912 (D4142) is seen as station pilot at Carlisle station. This loco carries BR blue livery, but has had a Transrail 'T' added to the battery box cover. This loco was sold to A.V. Dawson, Middlesbrough, as a source of spare parts for their other Class 08s.

No. 08914, 6 June 1987

No. 08914 (D4144) is seen stabled at Tinsley depot, Sheffield. This view shows the clean roof detail of the class. No. 08914 would be scrapped by Ron Hull Jr, Rotherham, in 2005.

No. 08920, 21 June 1989

No. 08920 (D4150) is seen carrying unbranded Railfreight livery at Bescot. This was a solid West Midlands loco, allocated at various times to Tyseley, Bescot and Saltley, only being transferred away in 2001 to Toton. It would even be scrapped in the West Midlands, with European Metal Recycling cutting up the loco in 2011.

No. 08927, 10 March 1996

No. 08927 (D4157) is seen acting as station pilot at Northampton while carrying BR blue livery. This loco would be sold to Traditional Traction and can be found working at Doncaster Roberts Road repot, carrying BR green livery.

No. 08928, 10 March 1996

No. 08928 (D4158) stands at Norwich Crown Point depot carrying original Railfreight livery, but with a blue stripe instead of red. The loco also carries large numbers on the battery box cover. This loco spent many years based in the West Midlands before being transferred to Norwich, but came back to the West Midlands for scrapping, when it was cut up by European Metal Recycling, Kingsbury, in 2010.

No. 08931, 27 October 1996

No. 08931 (D4161) is seen in storage at Thornaby depot, carrying BR blue livery. Upon withdrawal, this loco was sent to Ferrybridge depot to act as a mobile engine transporter and had most of its bodywork cut away. It was finally scrapped by Ron Hull Jr, Rotherham, in 2005.

No. 08936, 5 October 2003

No. 08936 (D4166) stands at Barrow Hill depot, carrying Harry Needle orange livery. This loco was sold to RMS Locotec and can today be found at the Weardale Railway.

No. 08941, 8 August 1992

No. 08941 (D4171) is seen at Laira depot, Plymouth, awaiting repairs. It is minus its coupling rods. This would be scrapped by C. F. Booth, Rotherham, in 2011.

D4173, 21 May 2000

D4173 (No. 08943) is seen in BR green livery at Crewe Works, awaiting its naming ceremony; it would be named *Pet II*. Today this loco works for Harry Needle and can be found at Central Rivers depot, Burton-on-Trent.

No. 08944, 8 July 2016

No. 08944 (D4174) undergoes repairs at Bury on the East Lancashire Railway. This loco carries black livery, and has been at the East Lancs Railway since 2000.

No. 08946, 29 April 1997

No. 08946 (D4176) is seen stabled at Saltley depot, Birmingham, carrying Railfreight Distribution livery, complete with red running numbers. Saltley had lost its allocation of shunters long before this photograph was taken, with Bescot taking over the shunter allocation for the West Midlands, although No. 08946 would later be reallocated to Allerton but remain out-based at Saltley. No. 08946 was scrapped at Rye Farm, Wishaw, in 2008.

No. 08947, 3 February 1991

No. 08947 (D4177) is seen stabled at Old Oak Common depot, carrying BR blue livery. This loco was later sold for industrial use and now works for Aggregate Industries Ltd based at Whatley Quarry.

No. 08953, 10 August 1987

No. 08953 (D4183) is seen stabled at Laira depot, Plymouth, carrying BR blue livery and the unofficial name *Plymouth*. No. 08953 would be scrapped by European Metal Recycling, Attercliffe, in 2012.

No. 08954, 3 December 1995

No. 08954 (D4184) is seen looking very smart at Cardiff Canton, having been recently repainted into Railfreight grey livery; it has had a Transrail 'T' added to the engine room doors. No. 08954 was later sold to Harry Needle, and today works at Edge Hill, Liverpool.

No. 08956, 1 July 1996

No. 08956 (D4187) brings a departmental working out of the RTC at Derby. The consist includes test cars and track machines. No. 08956 still works for Network Rail and can be found at the Old Dalby test track.

No. 08957, 3 August 1990

No. 08957 (D4191) is seen acting as station pilot at King's Cross station, London. The shunter was based here to shunt release the parcels locos before the opening of the Princess Royal Distribution Centre. No. 08957 would be scrapped by European Metal Recycling, Kingsbury, in 2004.

No. 09001, 14 September 1995

No. 09001 (D3665) runs light engine through Newport while carrying BR blue livery. The Class 09s differed from the Class 08s by having a higher top speed. Most of the class also carried high-level air pipes for use with Southern Region EMU stock, as most were first allocated to the Southern Region. No. 09001 was eventually preserved at Peak Rail, carrying EWS maroon livery.

No. 09002, 3 April 1976

No. 09002 (D3666) rests at Brighton while carrying BR blue livery. This loco was sold to the South Devon Railway for preservation, but was subsequently resold to GB Railfreight; it can be found shunting at Whitemoor yard.

No. 09005, 10 May 1992

No. 09005 (D3669) is seen stabled at Knottingley, having just been repainted into departmental grey livery. At this time most of the Class 09s were still allocated to the Southern Region, but a start was being made on moving them around the country.

No. 09010, 4 April 1976

No. 09010 (D3721) rests at Hither Green depot in London, carrying a fresh coat of BR blue livery. This view shows the high-level air pipes that were fitted to most of the Class 09s. No. 09010 would eventually find its way into preservation, and can be found at the South Devon Railway.

No. 09106, 23 August 2007

No. 09106 (D3927, No. 08759) is seen working through Doncaster station with an engineers' train. No. 09106 was rebuilt from No. 08759 by RFS Industries, Kilnhurst, in 1993. No. 09106 is still currently active in the EWS fleet, based at Knottingley, but has recently been put up for sale.

No. 09105, 4 August 1996

No. 09105 (D4003, No. 08835) is seen stabled at Cardiff Canton. This loco, like all the other rebuilds, carries departmental grey livery. The later rebuilds didn't carry the high-level air pipes, but were re-geared to have the same maximum speed. No. 09105 was rebuilt from No. 08835, and has since been scrapped by C. F. Booth, Rotherham, in 2011.

No. 09011, 28 April 1997

No. 09011 (D4099) is seen stabled at Saltley depot, Birmingham, carrying departmental grey livery. This loco carries the unofficial name *Sudbury*; it was allocated to Allerton at the time, but was outbased at Saltley. No. 09011 would be scrapped by European Metal Recycling, Kingsbury, in 2011.

D4100, 20 July 2016

D4100 (No. 09012) is seen preserved at Kidderminster on the Severn Valley Railway. This loco carries BR green livery and the name *Dick Hardy*, a name it had when in British Rail service.

No. 09013, 3 December 1995

No. 09013 (D4101) is seen stabled at Cardiff Canton while carrying departmental grey livery. This was one of the first Class 09s to leave the Southern Region, finding its way to Tinsley in 1989. The loco carries Railfreight Metals logos and also a Cardiff depot plaque. No. 09013 would be scrapped by C. F. Booth, Rotherham, in 2011.

No. 09015, 1 April 1997

No. 09015 (D4103) is seen at Newport stabling point. Today this point has been closed and the track lifted, while No. 09015 can be found at Rye Farm, Wishaw, where it is in a derelict state.

No. 09017, 4 June 2013

No. 09017 (D4105, No. 97806) is seen carrying maroon livery inside the National Railway Museum, York. This loco was reallocated from the Southern Region to Cardiff in 1987, and was outbased at Sudbrook pumping station for use on the Severn Tunnel emergency train, gaining the number 97806 in the process. It was later renumbered back to 09017, before being preserved at York.

No. 09018, 8 August 2013

No. 09018 (D4106) is seen at Horstead Keynes on the Bluebell Railway. No. 09018 was operated by Harry Needle, in whose livery it is seen. The livery is certainly bright, and the former HNRC logo can just be made out on the bodyside doors.

No. 09019, 13 May 2008

No. 09019 (D4107) is seen acting as yard pilot at Eastleigh. No. 09019 carries the remains of mainline blue livery, and looks in need of a repaint. Today No. 09019 has been preserved and can be found at the West Somerset Railway.

No. 09020, 3 April 1986

No. 09020 (D4108) is seen acting as yard pilot at Clapham Junction. At this time you could only find the Class 09s on the Southern Region before they started to be moved around to different depots off the region. No. 09020 would be scrapped by European Metal Recycling, Kingsbury, in 2012.

No. 09021, 15 January 2000

No. 09021 (D4109) is seen acting as yard pilot at Bescot, having not long being repainted into EWS maroon livery. Despite looking superb, No. 09021 would end up being scrapped by C. F. Booth, Rotherham, in 2008.

No. 09024, 16 April 2016

No. 09024 (D4112) is seen at Bury (Bolton Street) station on the East Lancashire Railway. The Class 09s are popular on preserved lines due to their higher speed. No. 09024 still carries former mainline blue livery. No. 09024, along with No. 09025, were delivered without the high-level air pipes, as they were not delivered to the Southern Region.

No. 09025, 30 April 2001

No. 09025 (D4113) rests at Brighton station in between shunt duties. At this time there were two Class 09s allocated to Brighton, which were used to shunt release the Virgin Trains Class 47s that arrived on CrossCountry duty. No. 09025 carries Connex livery, and was the only locomotive to do so. No. 09025 was saved for preservation and can be found at the Lavender Line.

No. 09026, 21 July 2016

No. 09026 (D4114) is seen preserved at Tunbridge Wells West on the Spa Valley Railway. This loco carries the name *Cedric Wares* and had just entered preservation, having been used by Southern at Lovers Lane depot, Brighton.

F202, 2 March 2010

F202 is seen in preservation at the Seymour Railway Heritage Centre, Victoria, Australia. The Class 08 design was sold to both Australia and the Netherlands, with sixteen examples finding their way down under. Today six are in preservation, with F202 carrying Victoria Railways blue livery. All were built at the Dick Kerr Works, Preston, from 1951 onwards.

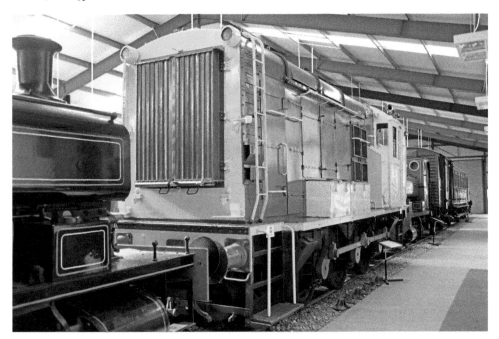

NS 601, 5 March 2016

NS 601 (NS 671) is seen in preservation at the Ribble Steam Railway. This loco was one of sixty-five built for use in the Netherlands, and was the first member built – there are currently seven members in the UK. It carried the number 671 when it was fitted with remote-control equipment. All of these locos were built either at the Dick Kerr Works in Preston or the English Electric Works at Newton-le-Willows from 1950 onwards.